Common Core
State

By Carole Marsh ©Carole Marsh/Gallopade
Published by Gallopade International, Inc.
Printed in the U.S.A. (Peachtree City, Georgia)

TABLE OF CONTENTS

G: Includes Graphic Organizer
GO: Graphic Organizer is also available 8½" x 11" online
        download at www.gallopade.com/client/go
(numbers above correspond to the graphic organizer numbers online)

What's the Matter?

Read the text and answer the questions.

Everything in the physical world around us is made up of either <u>matter</u> or <u>energy</u>.

You, the desk you are sitting at, the tree outside your window, the window—all of it is matter. If it has mass and takes up space, it is matter. The measurement for matter is mass. Mass describes how much matter an object contains. Heavier objects have more mass than lighter objects. Size alone does not determine matter because even though larger objects are often heavier than smaller objects, that is not always the case. Mass is measured in grams (g). One ounce is equal to 28.3495 grams.

Energy, on the other hand, is a force that can be used to move or change matter. You move matter when you use energy to throw a baseball. You change matter when you boil a pot of water and some of the water turns into steam. Heat, pressure, and a force of motion are some examples of types of energy.

1. A. Define <u>matter</u> and <u>energy</u> as they are used throughout the text.
   B. Explain how matter and energy are different.
   C. Explain how matter and energy are related.

2. Use information from the text to calculate how many grams are in a pound. (Hint: There are 16 ounces in a pound.)

3. Use examples in the text and your personal experiences to give three additional examples of energy being used to move or change matter.

4. Rank these objects based on their mass, with 1 having the least amount of matter and 5 having the most:

   _____Bird feather

   _____Mount Everest

   _____Basketball

   _____Circus elephant

   _____A book bag full of books

States of Matter

Read the text and answer the questions.

There are three classic states of matter: <u>solid</u>, <u>liquid</u>, and <u>gas</u>. Two of them, solid and liquid, are easy to see and identify. While gas can sometimes be seen, there are times it can only be identified by its smell or the effect it has on other matter.

Solids are hard and hold their shape, while liquids flow and take the shape of the container that holds them. Gases, such as oxygen, are everywhere around us. Gases don't have shape, but they still have mass.

A fourth state of matter, plasma, may not seem to be so common because it is rarely found on Earth, but it is actually the most common form of visible matter throughout the universe. Lightning, stars, and the aurora borealis, also known as the Northern Lights, are examples of plasmas.

A fifth state of matter was recently discovered—Bose-Einstein condensate, or "BEC." It doesn't exist naturally on our planet, and it only occurs in temperatures close to absolute zero. Absolute zero is the coldest temperature possible—here there is no heat or activity.

1. Use the text to complete the chart.

STATES OF MATTER	EXAMPLE OF EACH

2. Match the following questions to whether they are best answered by paragraph 1, 2, 3, or 4 of the text.
   A. _____How do states of matter behave?
   B. _____What is plasma?
   C. _____What are the three classic states of matter?

3. What can you infer about the characteristics of plasma based on the examples provided in the text?

4. Where do you think the fifth state of matter exists? Explain why.

Matter's Building Blocks

Read the text and answer the questions.

Matter is made up of atoms. Atoms are too small to be seen with the human eye or even a high-powered microscope. There are more than 100 known kinds of atoms, called <u>elements</u>. Atoms can be arranged in an infinite variety of combinations to produce all the objects around us. For that reason, atoms are known as the building blocks of matter. Atoms are similar to letters of the alphabet in that atoms can be combined to make matter, just as letters can be combined to make words.

While atoms are the basic units of matter, they are not the smallest particles. In fact, atoms are made up of tinier units. Every atom has a <u>nucleus</u> in the middle of it, much like our solar system has the sun at its center. The nucleus is made up of particles called <u>protons</u> and <u>neutrons</u>. Protons have positive charges, while neutrons have no charge.

Each element has a specific number of protons in its nucleus. The number of protons in an element's nucleus is the element's <u>atomic number</u>. For example, oxygen atoms have 8 protons, so oxygen's atomic number is 8.

Atoms also have <u>electrons</u>, negatively charged particles that orbit around the outside of the nucleus. When two or more atoms share electrons, they become bound together into <u>molecules</u>.

Molecules can be made up of atoms of the same element or different elements. Oxygen atoms can join together, or they can join with or other elements. The number and kind of atoms in a molecule is called its <u>chemical composition</u>. Molecules are the larger building blocks of matter, similar to how words are the building blocks used to make sentences.

PART A: Use the text to identify each statement as **true** or **false**.

1. _____ Molecules combine to create atoms.

2. _____ Protons have a positive charge.

3. _____ Every atom has a nucleus at its center.

4. _____ The number of elements is infinite.

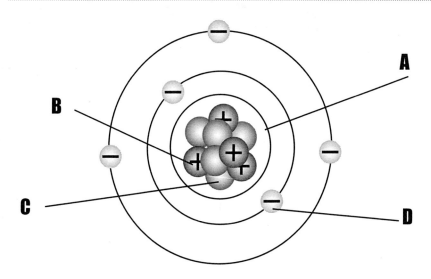

5. The drawing above is an illustration of_____.

6. A. What is marked with arrow A?
   B. What is marked with arrow B?
   C. What is marked with arrow C?
   D. What is marked with arrow D?

7. The item that is illustrated can combine with other items similar to it.
   A. When they combine, what binds them together?
   B. When they combine, what do they form?

8. Use details from the illustration and text to create an analogy between an atom and our solar system.

PART C: Use the text to answer the questions.

9. Define <u>element</u> as it is used in the text.

10. What two pieces of information are provided by a molecule's chemical composition?

11. If an atom has 2 protons in its nucleus, what is its atomic number?

12. Explain why atoms are called the "building blocks of matter."

Molecules Matter

Read the text and answer the questions.

> Molecules, and the atoms that make molecules, behave differently when they are in different states of matter. When molecules are very close together, like sardines in a can, they do not have much room to move. When molecules are spread out, like kindergartners going outside for recess, they can move around a lot.
>
> In a solid state of matter, molecules are very close to one another. Molecules in a solid are locked together in a tight pattern. While the molecules can vibrate, they do not move about freely.
>
> In a liquid state of matter, molecules have a bit more room to move and flow. They still hold together, but they can move and slide past one another. This motion explains why liquids do not have a sturdy shape and take the shape of their container.
>
> In a gas state of matter, molecules are very free to move around. As a gas, molecules can spread out to fill an entire area.

1. A. What two analogies are used in the text?
    B. What is the purpose of the analogies used in the text?

2. Use the three boxes below to illustrate the difference between molecules in different states of matter.
    A. Draw dots to represent molecules in a solid state in box 1.
    B. Draw dots to represent molecules in a liquid state in box 2.
    C. Draw dots to represent molecules in a gaseous state in box 3.

1	2	3

3. Why do liquids take the shape of their container?

4. Write a short journal entry describing an example of each state of matter in a way that you encounter it in your daily life. For each example, tell its state of matter and describe some of its characteristics, such as how it is contained and if and how it moves.

Feel the Heat

Read the text and answer the questions.

Heat is a form of energy. When heat is applied to or taken from matter, matter will be affected. If the temperature rises or drops a little, you may not see much of a change, but change the temperature enough to hit one of the "magic numbers," and the effect is remarkable.

Just what are these "magic numbers" that can have such a significant effect? They are the temperatures where matter changes from one state into another. Some of these "magic numbers" occur when matter is heated and some occur when matter is cooled.

• Every solid has a <u>melting point</u>. This is the temperature at which when lowered to, it will change from a solid into a liquid.

• Every liquid has a <u>boiling point</u>. This is the temperature at which when raised to, a liquid will become a gas.

• Every liquid also has a <u>freezing point</u>. This is the temperature at which when lowered to, it will change from a liquid into a solid.

• Every gas has a <u>condensation point</u>. This is the temperature at which when lowered to, it will change from a gas to a liquid.

An amazing thing about matter is that even when it changes its state, it is still made of the same elements! Whether it is in its solid, liquid, or gaseous state, water is still water. It still has the same chemical composition, no matter which state of matter it is in. This holds true for any substance.

1. A. Use the text to label each arrow with a + or – to designate that heat is added or taken away as it changes from one state to the other.
    B. Use the text to label each arrow with the name of the "magic number" the temperature must reach in order for the change from one state of matter to the other to occur.

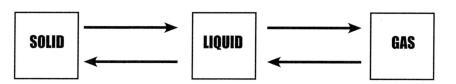

Solid State

Read the text and answer the questions.

Matter in its solid state holds its shape. A solid cannot be easily compressed. It might feel soft or stretchy, but its shape does not easily change unless it is cut or broken.

Matter that is not in a solid state can be changed into a solid state. A liquid can be changed into a solid state by being cooled until it reaches its freezing point. When the liquid is cooled, its atoms slow down and get closer together, and when it reaches the freezing point, it changes from liquid to solid. A gas can be changed into a solid state by first cooling it enough to change it into a liquid, and then cooling it to convert it into a solid.

Similarly, matter that is in a solid state can be changed into another state. When a solid is heated up to its melting point, the solid will become a liquid. The liquid can then be heated even more, and if it reaches its boiling point, it will become a gas.

In some cases, a solid can be changed directly into a gas without becoming a liquid first. This process is called <u>sublimation</u>. An example of sublimation is when dry ice goes directly from ice, a solid state, to mist, a gaseous state.

A solid can also be changed to a BEC by cooling it so much that it almost reaches absolute zero. This has only been done in a laboratory.

1. Give two characteristics of a solid.

2. What happens to a solid when it reaches its melting point?

3. What happens to atoms in a liquid when it is cooled?

4. Use the text to define <u>sublimation</u>.

5. Is a burning candle an example of sublimation? Why or why not?

6. How can a solid be changed into a BEC?

7. What is the role of temperature in changing matter from one state of matter to another? Cite information from the text to support your answer.

Liquids: Wet & Wild

Read the text and answer the questions.

When matter is in a liquid state, its atoms are able to move and slide around. However, they do not separate too far, because they are held together by <u>cohesion</u>. Cohesion is a force that binds the atoms to one another and prevents them from flying off. The atoms in liquids are not packed together as tightly as the atoms in solids, but they are not as free as the atoms are in gases. It is possible, but rather difficult, to compress liquids.

A liquid does not hold its own shape, but takes the shape of whatever container it is in. A liquid usually feels wet. Usually, a liquid can be poured. Some liquids are harder to pour than others. For example, honey is harder to pour than water. The resistance of a liquid to being poured is called its <u>viscosity</u>. Viscosity is determined by the size and complexity of the liquid's molecules. Honey has a higher viscosity than water, or is said to be more viscous.

A liquid can be changed to a solid state by being cooled until its atoms slow down, like when water is frozen into ice in a freezer. A liquid can also be heated up so much that its atoms speed up, causing the liquid to become a gas. The process of turning a liquid into a gas is called <u>vaporization</u>.

1. Use the text to define and give a synonym for each word:
   A. <u>cohesion</u>
   B. <u>viscosity</u>
   C. <u>vaporization</u>

2. What happens when a liquid is heated to its boiling point?

3. How can a liquid be turned into a solid?

4. What is the name of the process for changing a liquid to a gas?

5. Think of liquids you are familiar with and list two with a high viscosity.

6. Do you think there is a connection between how cohesive the atoms are in a liquid and how viscous the liquid is? Support your answer with at least two examples of liquids you are familiar with.

It's a Gas!

Read the text and answer the questions.

Gas is a state of matter that can be hard to see, but don't be fooled—gases are everywhere! The gases in our atmosphere make it possible for plants and animals to live. They also make it possible for birds and airplanes to fly.

A gas does not have its own shape or size, but it still has mass. That means, like all matter, a gas is made up of atoms. The atoms in a gas have lots of energy so they bounce around quickly and constantly. Atoms in a gas can move very far from one another, and they will spread out to fill up a container.

A gas can be changed into a liquid through compression, which is the use of high pressure. Compression forces the atoms in a gas closer together, causing them to slow down and change from a gas state into a liquid state.

A gas can also be changed into a liquid by lowering the temperature of the gas until it reaches its condensation point. An example of this is when the water vapor in clouds condenses so much that it becomes rain.

A gas can also be changed into plasma by subjecting it to very high temperatures or a huge difference in voltage between two points. Lightning is an example of this.

1. A. True or False: Because gases are invisible, they are unimportant.
   B. Cite evidence from the text to support your answer.

2. Why do atoms in gases bounce around so much?

3. Do gases have mass? Why or why not?

4. Compare and contrast compression and condensation, as they apply to the process of changing a gas into a liquid.

5. Complete the graphic organizer by adding the cause.

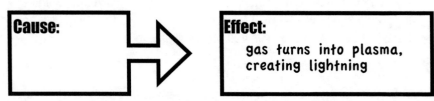

Cause:

Effect:
gas turns into plasma, creating lightning

Plasma

Read the text and complete the graphic organizer.

What is the most common state of visible matter throughout the universe? It is plasma! Plasma is visible in natural phenomena like the sun, stars, and lightning. Plasma is also visible in man-made creations such as neon signs and fluorescent lighting.

Atoms in plasma have a lot of the same qualities as the atoms in gases. They are full of energy, they do not hold their own shape or size, and they spread apart quickly. But unlike the atoms typical in a gas, plasma atoms are ions.

Most atoms have an equal number of protons, which have a positive charge and are found in the nucleus, and electrons, which have a negative charge and orbit the nucleus. Because of this equal combination, most atoms are said to have a neutral charge—their positive and negative charges are balanced out.

Ions are atoms that either have too many or too few electrons. If the ion has one or two extra electrons, it has a negative charge; if it is missing an electron or two, its charge is positive.

Atoms are always trying to stay balanced, or "happy." Ions attract each other so they can swap or share electrons to try and equal their protons with the number of electrons around them.

The effects of having ions give plasmas some interesting characteristics that gases do not have: plasmas conduct electricity and they produce magnetic forces and electric currents.

Use the Venn diagram to compare and contrast gases and plasmas.

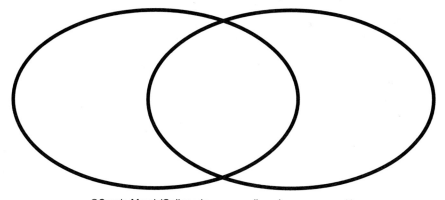

Wonderful Water

Read the text and answer the questions.

Have you ever heard of the molecule known as H_2O? This molecule is a compound made up of one oxygen atom and two hydrogen atoms. You know H_2O as water.

Water is the most commonly found compound on Earth. It covers more than 70% of our planet's surface. Water is found around the world in the classic three states of matter—solid, liquid, and gas. Water is most often seen in its liquid form, making liquid the most abundant state of matter on Earth.

We normally think of water in its liquid state in oceans, rivers, or as it rushes out of the faucet. Ice caps and glaciers are examples of water in its solid state. Clouds, steam, and mist are examples of water when it is in its gaseous state.

Whatever state it is in, the chemical composition of water is the same. It is still H_2O, so it is always water.

1. In the illustration of the water molecule, which circle(s) represent oxygen and which circle(s) represent hydrogen? Label them.

2. How does the chemical composition of water change when water changes from one state of matter to another?

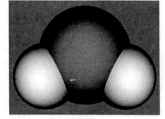

Water Molecule

3. A. If another oxygen atom combined with a water molecule, would the new molecule still be water? Why or why not?
   B. Write the chemical composition of the new molecule.

4. Use magazines or other sources to find photographs of water in each of its three natural states of matter. Write a paragraph about water to go with each photograph. Identify the state of matter and describe the characteristics of water in that state. Be creative and use strong word choices to create multi-sensory descriptions.

Changing States of Matter

Conduct the experiment and answer the questions.
Note: Adult supervision required.

Materials Needed:

approximately 1 quart of water in a small pitcher or bowl
ice tray • pan with a lid • freezer • stove
pencil • paper

Procedure:

1. Look at the water in the pitcher or bowl.
   Record a description of the water.

2. Pour the water into the ice tray and place it in the freezer for 4 hours or more. After 4 hours, remove the ice tray from the freezer.
   Record a description of the water.

3. Remove the water from the ice tray and put it into the pan.
   Heat the water on low heat on the stove for 5 minutes.
   Record a description of the water and what you saw occur.

4. Heat the water on high heat on the stove for 5-10 minutes.
   Record a description of the water and what you saw occur.

5. Put the lid on the pan and boil the water on high heat on the stove for 1-2 minutes. Turn the heat off. Carefully lift the lid and look at the underneath side of it.
   Record a description of the water and what you saw occur.

1. Identify the state(s) of matter you observed at each step.

2. A. Identify the step(s) at which water reached any of these points:
       • boiling point   • condensation point
       • freezing point   • melting point
    B. For each time you identified a point in part A, indicate whether the temperature of the water was increasing or decreasing.
    C. For each time you identified a point in part A, describe the change that occurred in the water's state of matter (from _____ to _____).

3. Analyze your data to draw conclusions about water, states of matter, points at which water changes its states of matter, or anything else you determine. Write your conclusions in complete sentences.

BEC

Read the text and follow the instructions.

> The Bose-Einstein condensate, or BEC for short, is a "new" state of matter. It is not really new since it probably has always existed in the universe, but it is new to us because we did not know it existed until recently. Why did we not know about this state of matter? Because it cannot exist naturally on our planet.
>
> Scientists Satyendra Nath Bose and Albert Einstein predicted the existence of BEC in approximately 1925. Two other scientists, Eric Cornell and Carl Wieman, produced the first gaseous condensate in a laboratory in 1995. It was such an important accomplishment that they received the Nobel Prize for Physics in 2001. In 2010, the first photon BEC was observed.
>
> If plasma is a super-excited gas, then BEC is at the other end of the spectrum. BEC is a solid with atoms that are almost completely still. The BEC state of matter occurs when the atoms in a solid are cooled so intensely that they almost completely stop vibrating. That only happens near absolute zero. Since temperatures on Earth don't get that low, BEC was a state of matter that was conceived by scientists before it could be achieved.
>
> Scientists have theorized that there may be other states of matter in the universe that are unable to exist on Earth. Supersolids and dark matter are hypothetical examples.

1. Tap into your imagination and imagine a new state of matter. Where would you find it? What would it look like? What would it feel like? What other characteristics would it have? How would matter get to this state? What would it be called? Answer these and other questions in an informative essay about your newly discovered state of matter. Include an illustration or other visuals about your new state of matter. If desired, share your discovery with your class.

2. Albert Einstein once said, "The true sign of intelligence is not knowledge but imagination." How do you think imagination helps scientists develop theories? Can imagination help them test their theories too? Explain.

States of Matter

Compare and contrast the three classic states of matter.

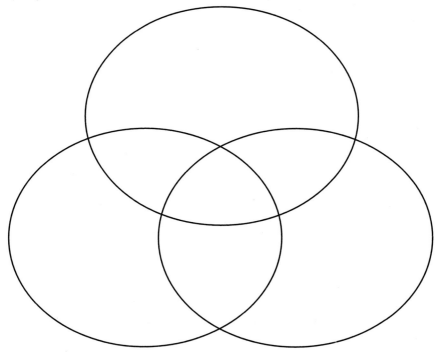

Compare and contrast plasma and BEC.

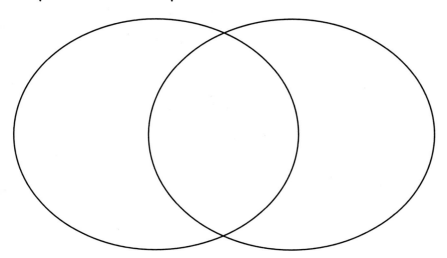

Mix Things Up

Read the text and answer the questions.

Mixtures are substances that are made up of more than one element or compound. In mixtures, the molecules of the elements or compounds are near each other but they do not change one another. In mixtures, the elements or compounds that combined to form the mixture can be separated back to their original forms. In other words, mixtures do not have to stay mixed forever.

Mixtures can be any state of matter. The substances combined to create a mixture do not have to be of the same state of matter. For example, salt (a solid) can be combined with water (a liquid) to make salt water. Salt water is a mixture.

Mixtures can be found everywhere. If you combine your dirty clothes with your sister's dirty clothes, you have created a mixture of dirty clothes. The mixture of clothes can still be separated back into your clothes and your sister's clothes.

Some mixtures are as easy to separate back into the original items as a load of dirty laundry. Other mixtures may require special tools or complex processes. However, in any mixture, the elements or compounds that were combined to form the mixture can be separated back into the original elements or compounds. That is because the things combined in a mixture do not have a chemical reaction, meaning their chemical structure does not change.

1. A. Use the text to write a scientific definition of mixture.
   B. Use the text to write an informal or everyday definition of mixture.

2. What makes a mixture a mixture? Use the text to create a list of important characteristics that all mixtures have.

3. Think of mixtures that you see or may be familiar with in your life.
   A. Give two examples of mixtures that are easily separated back into their original parts.
   B. Give two examples of mixtures that are NOT easily separated back into their original parts.

Find the Solution

Read the text and answer the questions.

Solutions are a type of mixture. In a solution, the molecules of the substances that were combined are evenly distributed throughout the mixture. There are no areas of the mixture where there is more or less of any of the substances compared to other areas of the mixture. Solutions are called homogenous mixtures.

There are many different types of solutions. Gases can be combined with solids, liquids, or other gases. Liquids can be combined with solids, gases, or other liquids. And solids can be combined with gases, liquids, or other solids.

A simple solution, like water and sugar, is the combination of two substances. In most simple solutions, at least one of the substances is in a liquid state when the mixture is made.

1. Use the text to define and describe key characteristics of solutions.

2. Explain the relationship between solutions and mixtures.

3. What can you infer about the meaning of homogenous from the text?

4. What conclusions can you draw from the text about the states of matter of mixtures?

5. List two characteristics typical of a simple solution.

6. For each mixture below, use the text and what you know, plus logical thinking, to decide if the mixture is a solution. Explain your reasoning for each answer.
   A. a mixture of salt and water
   B. a mixture of sand and water
   C. a glass of lemonade
   D. a bag of M&Ms

7. Use an online resource to write a definition and find an example of each of these special kinds of mixtures:
   A. alloy   B. amalgam   C. colloid   D. emulsion

Compounds

Read the text and answer the questions.

Sometimes the molecules of two or more elements come together and do not simply coexist beside one another. In some cases, a chemical reaction occurs and the molecules combine to create something new. This new substance is called a <u>compound</u>. Compounds are made when there is a change in the chemical structure of the elements and the substances become bonded.

When hydrogen and oxygen come together, the molecules bind together in a fixed pattern and become the compound H_2O, or hydrogen oxide, which we commonly refer to as water. The only way to separate the molecules of water, or any compound, is through a chemical process.

1. Use the text to define <u>compound</u>.

2. Many of the basic substances around us are compounds. Research the common names of these chemical compounds:

    $NaCl$ _____

    $CaCO_3$ _____

    FeO_2 _____

    CO_2 _____

    NH_3 _____

    SiO_2 _____

    $C1_2H_{22}O_{11}$ _____

3. Identify each of the following as either a compound or a mixture.

    H_2O _____

    $N_2 + O_2$ _____

    CH_4 _____

Mixture or Compound?

Read the text and answer the questions.

_____	Pour the contents of the glass into the pan and heat the pan on the stove.
_____	Adult supervision is required.
_____	small pan
_____	stove
_____	Boil off all the water.
_____	Record your observations.
_____	When water and salt are combined, is the result a compound or a mixture?
_____	glass of water
_____	spoon
_____	Add two tablespoons of salt to the glass of water and stir rapidly.
_____	table salt

1. The text for the experiment above has been jumbled up. Follow these steps to identify the various parts of the experiment.
   A. Identify the "Materials Required" with an "M."
   B. Identify important safety instructions with an "I."
   C. Identify the question the experiment should answer with a "Q."
   D. Identify the steps in the experiment with an "S."
   E. Number the steps 1-4 in the order they should occur.

2. When John did this experiment, his observation notes said, "When I finished boiling the contents of the glass, there was salt in the bottom and on the sides of the pan." Based on John's observation, what conclusions would you make? Explain why.

Scientists Who Matter

Use the text to match each photograph with the quotation that best fits the scientist(s) pictured.

The Indian scientist <u>Satyendra Nath Bose</u>, 1894-1974, was a multilingual scholar whose work in quantum mechanics in the 1920s helped provide the theoretical foundation for BEC, or Bose-Einstein condensate. Boson particles are named for him.

<u>Eric Cornell and Carl Wieman</u>, two American physicists born in the mid-1900s, synthesized the first BEC at a laboratory in 1995. They received the Nobel Prize in Physics in 2001 for their work.

<u>Lord Kelvin</u> lived in England from 1824-1907. He calculated absolute zero correctly, and the Kelvin measurements of temperature are named in his honor.

<u>Robert Boyle</u>, an Irishman who lived from 1627-1691, is considered to be the first modern chemist. He studied matter and made the distinction between mixtures and compounds.

The American scientist <u>Irving Langmuir</u>, 1881-1957, worked in chemistry and physics. He gave the fourth state of matter the name "plasma" because he said that the ionized gases reminded him of blood plasma.

Englishman <u>John Dalton</u> was a chemist, meteorologist, and physicist who lived from 1766-1844. He is known for his pioneering work in atomic theory.

Born in 1879 in Germany, <u>Albert Einstein</u> is one of the most well-known and respected scientists of the 20th century. He developed the theory of relativity and is responsible for the calculation $E=mc^2$. His theories helped in the discovery of BEC.

Sir <u>William Crookes</u> was born in England and lived from 1832 to 1919. He thought he had discovered a fourth state of matter, which he called "radiant matter." Other scientists continued his research, and we now know the fourth state of matter as plasma.

1. J. Dalton

2. S.N. Bose

3. I. Langmuir

4. Lord Kelvin

5. E. Cornell & C. Wieman

Photo by Ken Abbott

6. W. Crookes

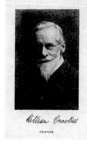

7. A. Einstein

8. R. Boyle

_____ "I gave the fourth state of matter the name of plasma because it reminded me of blood plasma."

_____ "We proved that the BEC state of matter does exist when we produced it in a laboratory."

_____ "I was one of the first scientists to observe the fourth state of matter. At that time, I called it radiant matter."

_____ "When scientists measure absolute zero, they use the thermal units that are named after me."

_____ "I am known for developing the theory of relativity, but BEC bears my name because of my theoretical contributions."

_____ "My interest was in atomic theory, even though I was born in the 1700s, well before the atomic age."

_____ "Boson particles are named for me, and my research in quantum mechanics helped in the discovery of BEC."

_____ "I studied matter and made the distinction between mixtures and compounds."

States of Matter

Fill in the chart with the definition for each word. Then number the words in alphabetical order.

Word		Definition
matter		
energy		
mass		
solid		
liquid		
gas		
plasma		
BEC		
absolute zero		
atom		
molecule		
nucleus		
proton		

Word		Definition
neutron		
electron		
ion		
melting point		
boiling point		
freezing point		
condensation point		
sublimation		
viscosity		
vaporization		
compression		
cohesion		
mixture		
solution		
compound		

Correlations to Common Core State Standards

For your convenience, correlations are listed page-by-page, and for the entire book!

This book is correlated to the Common Core State Standards for English Language Arts grades 3-8, and to Common Core State Standards for Literacy in History, Science, & Technological Subjects grades 6-8.

Correlations are highlighted in gray.

	READING	WRITING	LANGUAGE	SPEAKING & LISTENING
	Includes: RI: Reading Informational Text RST: Reading Science & Technical Subjects	**Includes:** W: Writing WHST: Writing History/Social Studies, Science, & Technical Subjects	**Includes:** L: Language LF: Language Foundational Skills	**Includes:** SL: Speaking & Listening
PAGE #				
2	RI · 1 2 3 4 5 6 7 8 9 10 RST	W · 1 2 3 4 5 6 7 8 9 10 WHST	L · 1 2 3 4 5 6 LF	SL · 1 2 3 4 5 6
3	RI · 1 2 3 4 5 6 7 8 9 10 RST	W · 1 2 3 4 5 6 7 8 9 10 WHST	L · 1 2 3 4 5 6 LF	SL · 1 2 3 4 5 6
4-5	RI · 1 2 3 4 5 6 7 8 9 10 RST	W · 1 2 3 4 5 6 7 8 9 10 WHST	L · 1 2 3 4 5 6 LF	SL · 1 2 3 4 5 6
6	RI · 1 2 3 4 5 6 7 8 9 10 RST	W · 1 2 3 4 5 6 7 8 9 10 WHST	L · 1 2 3 4 5 6 LF	SL · 1 2 3 4 5 6
7	RI · 1 2 3 4 5 6 7 8 9 10 RST	W · 1 2 3 4 5 6 7 8 9 10 WHST	L · 1 2 3 4 5 6 LF	SL · 1 2 3 4 5 6
8	RI · 1 2 3 4 5 6 7 8 9 10 RST	W · 1 2 3 4 5 6 7 8 9 10 WHST	L · 1 2 3 4 5 6 LF	SL · 1 2 3 4 5 6
9	RI · 1 2 3 4 5 6 7 8 9 10 RST	W · 1 2 3 4 5 6 7 8 9 10 WHST	L · 1 2 3 4 5 6 LF	SL · 1 2 3 4 5 6
10	RI · 1 2 3 4 5 6 7 8 9 10 RST	W · 1 2 3 4 5 6 7 8 9 10 WHST	L · 1 2 3 4 5 6 LF	SL · 1 2 3 4 5 6
11	RI · 1 2 3 4 5 6 7 8 9 10 RST	W · 1 2 3 4 5 6 7 8 9 10 WHST	L · 1 2 3 4 5 6 LF	SL · 1 2 3 4 5 6
12	RI · 1 2 3 4 5 6 7 8 9 10 RST	W · 1 2 3 4 5 6 7 8 9 10 WHST	L · 1 2 3 4 5 6 LF	SL · 1 2 3 4 5 6
13	RI · 1 2 3 4 5 6 7 8 9 10 RST	W · 1 2 3 4 5 6 7 8 9 10 WHST	L · 1 2 3 4 5 6 LF	SL · 1 2 3 4 5 6
14	RI · 1 2 3 4 5 6 7 8 9 10 RST	W · 1 2 3 4 5 6 7 8 9 10 WHST	L · 1 2 3 4 5 6 LF	SL · 1 2 3 4 5 6
15	RI · 1 2 3 4 5 6 7 8 9 10 RST	W · 1 2 3 4 5 6 7 8 9 10 WHST	L · 1 2 3 4 5 6 LF	SL · 1 2 3 4 5 6
16	RI · 1 2 3 4 5 6 7 8 9 10 RST	W · 1 2 3 4 5 6 7 8 9 10 WHST	L · 1 2 3 4 5 6 LF	SL · 1 2 3 4 5 6
17	RI · 1 2 3 4 5 6 7 8 9 10 RST	W · 1 2 3 4 5 6 7 8 9 10 WHST	L · 1 2 3 4 5 6 LF	SL · 1 2 3 4 5 6
18	RI · 1 2 3 4 5 6 7 8 9 10 RST	W · 1 2 3 4 5 6 7 8 9 10 WHST	L · 1 2 3 4 5 6 LF	SL · 1 2 3 4 5 6
19	RI · 1 2 3 4 5 6 7 8 9 10 RST	W · 1 2 3 4 5 6 7 8 9 10 WHST	L · 1 2 3 4 5 6 LF	SL · 1 2 3 4 5 6
20-21	RI · 1 2 3 4 5 6 7 8 9 10 RST	W · 1 2 3 4 5 6 7 8 9 10 WHST	L · 1 2 3 4 5 6 LF	SL · 1 2 3 4 5 6
22-23	RI · 1 2 3 4 5 6 7 8 9 10 RST	W · 1 2 3 4 5 6 7 8 9 10 WHST	L · 1 2 3 4 5 6 LF	SL · 1 2 3 4 5 6
COMPLETE BOOK	RI · 1 2 3 4 5 6 7 8 9 10 RST	W · 1 2 3 4 5 6 7 8 9 10 WHST	L · 1 2 3 4 5 6 LF	SL · 1 2 3 4 5 6

For the complete Common Core standard identifier, combine your grade + "." + letter code above + "." + number code above.

In addition to the correlations indicated here, the activities may be adapted or expanded to align to additional standards and to meet the diverse needs of your unique students!

Correlations to Common Core State Standards

For your convenience, correlations are listed page-by-page, and for the entire book!

This book is correlated to the <u>Common Core State Standards for English Language Arts</u> grades 3-8, and to <u>Common Core State Standards for Literacy in History, Science, & Technological Subjects</u> grades 6-8.

Correlations are highlighted in gray.

	READING	WRITING	LANGUAGE	SPEAKING & LISTENING
	Includes: RI: Reading Informational Text RST: Reading Science & Technical Subjects	**Includes:** W: Writing WHST: Writing History/Social Studies, Science, & Technical Subjects	**Includes:** L: Language LF: Language Foundational Skills	**Includes:** SL: Speaking & Listening

PAGE #	RI / RST	W / WHST	L / LF	SL
2	1 2 3 4 5 6 7 8 9 10	1 2 3 4 5 6 7 8 9 10	1 2 3 4 5 6	1 2 3 4 5 6
3	1 2 3 4 5 6 7 8 9 10	1 2 3 4 5 6 7 8 9 10	1 2 3 4 5 6	1 2 3 4 5 6
4	1 2 3 4 5 6 7 8 9 10	1 2 3 4 5 6 7 8 9 10	1 2 3 4 5 6	1 2 3 4 5 6
5	1 2 3 4 5 6 7 8 9 10	1 2 3 4 5 6 7 8 9 10	1 2 3 4 5 6	1 2 3 4 5 6
6	1 2 3 4 5 6 7 8 9 10	1 2 3 4 5 6 7 8 9 10	1 2 3 4 5 6	1 2 3 4 5 6
7	1 2 3 4 5 6 7 8 9 10	1 2 3 4 5 6 7 8 9 10	1 2 3 4 5 6	1 2 3 4 5 6
8-9	1 2 3 4 5 6 7 8 9 10	1 2 3 4 5 6 7 8 9 10	1 2 3 4 5 6	1 2 3 4 5 6
10-11	1 2 3 4 5 6 7 8 9 10	1 2 3 4 5 6 7 8 9 10	1 2 3 4 5 6	1 2 3 4 5 6
12-13	1 2 3 4 5 6 7 8 9 10	1 2 3 4 5 6 7 8 9 10	1 2 3 4 5 6	1 2 3 4 5 6
14-15	1 2 3 4 5 6 7 8 9 10	1 2 3 4 5 6 7 8 9 10	1 2 3 4 5 6	1 2 3 4 5 6
16	1 2 3 4 5 6 7 8 9 10	1 2 3 4 5 6 7 8 9 10	1 2 3 4 5 6	1 2 3 4 5 6
17	1 2 3 4 5 6 7 8 9 10	1 2 3 4 5 6 7 8 9 10	1 2 3 4 5 6	1 2 3 4 5 6
18	1 2 3 4 5 6 7 8 9 10	1 2 3 4 5 6 7 8 9 10	1 2 3 4 5 6	1 2 3 4 5 6
19	1 2 3 4 5 6 7 8 9 10	1 2 3 4 5 6 7 8 9 10	1 2 3 4 5 6	1 2 3 4 5 6
20-21	1 2 3 4 5 6 7 8 9 10	1 2 3 4 5 6 7 8 9 10	1 2 3 4 5 6	1 2 3 4 5 6
22	1 2 3 4 5 6 7 8 9 10	1 2 3 4 5 6 7 8 9 10	1 2 3 4 5 6	1 2 3 4 5 6
23	1 2 3 4 5 6 7 8 9 10	1 2 3 4 5 6 7 8 9 10	1 2 3 4 5 6	1 2 3 4 5 6
COMPLETE BOOK	1 2 3 4 5 6 7 8 9 10	1 2 3 4 5 6 7 8 9 10	1 2 3 4 5 6	1 2 3 4 5 6

For the complete Common Core standard identifier, combine your grade + "." + letter code above + "." + number code above.

In addition to the correlations indicated here, the activities may be adapted or expanded to align to additional standards and to meet the diverse needs of your unique students!

Land & Water Formations

Read the vocabulary definitions and answer the questions.

Isthmus—a strip of land that connects two larger pieces of land with water on two sides

Strait— a narrow passage of water that connects two larger bodies of water

Delta—a fan-shaped area of land or soil deposited at the mouth of a river

Peninsula—land that juts out into an ocean or sea so that it has water on three sides

Island—an area of land surrounded by water on all sides

Archipelago—a group of islands

Bay—a large body of water connected to a sea or ocean, but with land mostly surrounding it

Inlet—narrow strip of water that juts into coastline

1. A. Which of these might be described as a land formation?
    B. Which of these might be described as a water formation?

2. Use the definitions to identify each land and water formation labeled on the diagram.

A. _____   E. _____
B. _____   F. _____
C. _____   G. _____
D. _____   H. _____

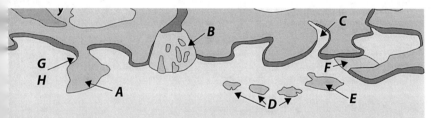

Research & Presentation: Working in pairs, use an online resource to research one of the following geographical locations. Create a digital presentation or visual poster to show where it is located on the Earth and how the land/water fits its definition. Give your presentation to the class.

**Strait of Gibraltar • Nile River Delta • Isthmus of Panama
Hudson Bay • Iberian Peninsula • Malay Archipelago**